Options Trading Strategies

The Simplified Guide For Beginners To Learn the Bases of Investing, Make Profits With Popular Options Strategies And Generate Passive Income.

Byron McGrady

Table of Contents

Introduction

If you have heard about the world of options trading, you might be wondering what investment you can make with options. You can make money out of trading options with anyone, whether you are a complete beginner or an experienced trader.

This is for those who are yet to find out about the market and are unsure how it all works. You will learn the market and how much profit can be made as a beginner.

The name "Options Trading" might make it sound like a complicated process, but that's far from the truth. The options market has been known for years and remains one of the most profitable and exciting investment opportunities available to us today. With technology constantly being developed, it's now easier than ever to trade options without worrying about complicated strategies or trading platforms.

A basic understanding of options will help you decide whether this is the right investment for you or not. As a beginner, it is easy to get lost in the world of finance and move into investing without knowing the basics.

Options are very different from stocks since they're designed as derivatives. That means that options are tied to an underlying asset (stock, index, or commodity) and are traded outside of their relationship with that asset. They're considered more speculative than conservative investments.

Stocks were designed as equity investments, which means that they represent ownership in the firms that issue them. Even though you can't cash out your shares before they mature, they provide a reliable way to earn passive income.

This explains how, as an options trader, one can gain passive income. It is possible by using different strategies while trading options and also making profits through this. The strategies explained here are tested as profitable in the market, but one should apply common sense.

Options are a very popular and effective way to make money. However, options trading has become extremely complicated and complex over the years. In this *Options Trading for Beginners*, we'll show you step by step how to start your investment journey.

Investors use options to speculate whether they believe that a stock's price will go up over time. If the investor anticipates that stock to increase, they will buy an option to gain exposure to that increase. If they do not predict that the price will increase, they may sell their option.

If you're new to the world of options trading, there are a few things that you need to know before you begin trading. You have to learn the basics of options trading at the outset before moving on to a more detailed explanation of each option's characteristics.

Remember this is not a complete guide on options trading. It is intended to give you a general idea of how options trading works. Before you begin trading options, it's important to know a little about what they are and how they work.

CHAPTER 1:

What Are Options?

An option is a financial contract called a derivative contract. It allows the owner of the agreement to have the right to buy or sell the securities based on an agreed-upon price by a specified period.

As the name suggests, there is no obligation in this type of transaction. The trader pays for the right or the option to buy or sell a purchase such as security, stock, index, or ETF (exchange-traded fund) by a certain amount of time. An alternative is a contract.

The option derives its value based on the value of the underlying asset, hence the term derivative contract. This contract states that the buyer agrees to purchase a specified asset within a certain amount of time at a prior agreed-upon price.

Derivative contracts are often used for commodities like gold, oil, and currencies, usually in US dollars. Another type of derivative based on the value of stocks and bonds. They can also find interest rates such as the yield on a specified amount of time, as a ten-year Treasury note.

In a derivative contract, the seller does not have to own the specified asset. They have to have enough money to cover the asset's price to fulfill the contract. The seller also can give the buyer another derivative contract to offset the asset's value.

An option contract usually contains the following specifications:

Agreed-Upon Price

Also known as the strike price. It does not change no matter how much time has passed, and it is so named because the trader strikes when the underlying value makes the desired income.

Specified Time

Also known as the expiration dates. This is the date at which the option (contract) expires. The trader can exercise the option at the strike price at any time up until the expiry date reaches. In some countries, such as Europe, a trader can only exercise the right to the option at the strike price exactly on the expiry date. We will more largely focus on the American way of trading options, which allows for exercising right on.

Rights Acquired With the Purchase of an Option

They can be call (right of purchase) and put (right of sale).

Trading options and trading stocks are different because stocks and options have different characteristics. Stocks stand for shares of ownership in individual companies or opportunities. It allows the stock trader to bet in any direction that they feel the stock price headed.

Stocks are an excellent investment if you think of long-term yields, such as for retirement and have the capital. They are very simplistic in the approach in that the trader buys the stock and wagers on the price they think will rise at a particular time in the future. The hope is that the price will increase in value, thus gaining the trader a substantial yield.

Stocks are an excellent option for those who want to invest without keeping a steady eye on the growth of the investment.

The risk of investing in stocks is that the price of shares can plummet to zero at any moment. It means that the investor can lose their entire investment at the drop of a hat because stocks are very volatile today. They are very reactive to world events such as wars, politics, scandals, epidemics, and natural disasters.

On the other hand, options are an excellent option for traders who would like flexibility with timing and risks. The trader is under no obligation and can see how the trade plays out over the time specified by the option contract. In that period, the price is locked, which is also a great appeal.

Trading options also require a lower investment compared to stocks typically.

Another excellent appeal for options trading is that the specified time is typically shorter than investing in stocks. For regular buying and selling as options have different expiration dates. Expiration dates extent from just a few days to several years.

The drawback that makes some people hesitate in trading options is that it is more complicated than trading stocks. The trader needs to learn new jargon and vocabulary such as strike prices, calls and puts to determine how they can set up effective options. Not only does the trader have to learn new terms, but they also have to develop new skillsets and the right mindset for options trading.

CHAPTER 2:

What Is Options Trading?

Trading options may seem overwhelming in the beginning, but it's easy to learn some key points. Investor portfolios are generally made up of different asset classes. These can be bonds, securities, mutual funds, and ETFs. Options are also asset class and, if used correctly, offer many benefits that trading in securities and ETFs alone cannot offer.

Options are contracts whereby the holder is entitled, but not required, to buy or sell an amount of the underlying asset at a default price before the contract's expiry. Options with brokerage investment accounts may be purchased as most other asset classes.

The options are powerful since they can improve the portfolio of an individual. You do this by adding income, protection, and even leveraging. Usually, a scenario corresponds to the investment goal depending on the situation. A common example would be the use of optional measures as an effective way to hide downside losses from a declining stock market. You may also use the options to generate recurring income. They are usually used for speculative purposes, for example. Bet on title direction.

There are no free stock and bond lunches. The options are no different. Trading options involve certain risks that investors need to be aware of. For this reason, when exchanging options with a broker, a disclaimer typically looks like this:

Options as Derivatives

The options belong to the largest group of securities called derivatives. The price of one derivative depends on or is derived from the price of another. For example, wine is a grape derivative, ketchup is a tomato derivative, and a stock option is a stock derivative. Options are financial instrument derivatives—their interest depends on the price of another currency. Calls, puts, futures, forward, swaps, and mortgage-backed securities are examples of derivatives.

Call and Put Options

Options are derived from a security type. An option is a derivative since its price is inseparable from the price of such goods. You are entitled but not obligated to buy or sell the assets underlying the contract at certain dates or before fixed prices.

The buyer has a right to purchase interest, and the investor can sell an interest. Imagine the future deposit of a call option.

Example of a Call Option

A potential homeowner sees new development. This person may wish to have the right to buy a home in the future but will not want to exercise that right until certain developments have developed in the area.

The prospective homebuyer would benefit from the purchase option or not. Imagine being able to purchase a call option from the developer to buy the house anytime in the next three years, for example, $400,000. Well, you can—it is a non-refundable deposit. Of course, the developer would not grant this option free. The prospective homebuyer needs to deposit to secure this right.

These costs are referred to as premium concerning an option. This is the cost of the contract for the option. The down payment the buyer pays the developer in our home example may amount to $20,000. It is now two years since the developments have gone and zoning has been approved. The homebuyer exercises this option, and the house is purchased for $400,000.

The market value of this home could have doubled to $800,000. However, since the deposit is tied to a fixed price, the buyer pays $400,000. For example, in an alternative scenario, zoning approval is not granted until the fourth year. This is one year after the expiration of this option. Now the homebuyer has to pay the market price because the contract has expired. Either way, the developer keeps the $20,000 originally raised.

Example of a Put Option

Now imagine an insurance policy option. You probably know how to take homeowners' insurance if you own your home. A homeowner purchases a homeowner protection policy against damage. For a period, say a year, you are paying a sum called a premium. In cases where the house is damaged, it has a nominal value and protects the policyholder.

What if your wealth was not a house but a capital stock or indexed investment? An investor will buy options when they need the S&P 500 index protection. An investor may be afraid a bear market is close and unable to lose over 10% of their long S&P 500 position. If the S&P 500 has a trade of $220, it can acquire the put option, for example, to sell the index at $2,250 for the next couple of years.

If the market collapses 20% over the next six months (500 index points), then a combined loss of only 10% will result in a 250-point scale of $2,250 at trading at $2,000. The loss would only be 10% if this option were kept, even if the market dropped to zero. Also, in this case, it is expensive (prime) to purchase the option. If the market does not drop, the maximum loss of option is only the premium paid.

You can do with the options four things:

- Buy calls.

- Sell calls.

- Buy puts.

- Sell puts.

Buying stocks gives you a long position. Buying a call option offers a potential long position in the underlying security. Short sales of stock give you a short position. If you sell an uncovered or uncovered call, you get a potential short position in the underlying action.

Buying a put option offers a potential short position in the underlying security. If you sell a naked or unmarried put, you get a potential long position in the title below. It is essential to keep these four scenarios clear.

People who buy options are called owners, and those who sell options are called option authors. This is the major difference between owners and authors:

Call holders and customers are not allowed to purchase or sell. You have the chance to exercise your rights. This limits the risk of option buyers to justify the premium.

However, Call Writer and Put Writer (seller) must buy or sell if the option expires in cash (more information below).

This means that a seller may have to keep a promise to buy or sell. This also means that sellers are exposed to greater and, sometimes, limitless risks. This means that authors can lose far more than the price of premium options.

Why Uses the Options?

Speculation

The future direction of the price is the bet on speculation. A speculator could believe that security prices would increase probably based on fundamental analysis or technical analysis. A speculator can buy the stock or purchase the inventory call option. It is interesting for some traders to specify a call option rather than purchasing the inventory directly because it leverages options. A money-free call will cost just a few bucks or even cents compared with the full price of a 100 bucks allocation.

Validation

The options were developed for hedging purposes. Hedging with options is designed to reduce risk at a reasonable cost. We should find solutions here like a scheme on insurance. As you insure your home or car, you can take the options to protect your investment from the recession.

Imagine wanting to buy tech stocks. Your losses, too, are restricted. You can limit your downside risk and take full advantage of all the advantages by using put options. Call options for short-sellers can be used to limit losses, especially in a shorter compression, when they are wrong.

CHAPTER 3:

Options Trading Basics

The options contract has an expiration date, depending on what type of options you are using. It may be in weeks, months, or even in years, unlike stock with no expiration date. Numbers usually define stocks, but on the other hand, there are no numbers in options.

Options drive their value from something else. That's why they fall into the derivative category, unlike stocks.

Stock owners have their right to the company (dividend or voting). On the other hand, options have no right in the company.

Some people may find it challenging to understand the option method though they have even followed it in their other transactions (car insurance or mortgages).

Few things make the difference between options trading and stock trading:

- In options trading, the value is taken by someone else and had a contract with it. It does not get the values on its own. This is entirely different from stock trading. Option trading belongs to the derivative category.

- In stock, the numbers are definite, but an option, the numbers are not definite.

- The options trading uses the contract, which has the expiration date; the person has no meaning after the expiry date. The date can be in months or years according to the option there are using. Stock trading has no expiration dates.

- In options trading, the owner has no right to the company. They have no affair of any kind related to the company. In stock share, they had the rights to the company.

Options trading may not suit all types of investors, but they are among the most flexible investment choices.

Options in investment are most likely used to reduce the risk of a drop in stock prices, but a little risk is involved in every investment type. Returns are never certain when investors look for options to control risks for ways to limit a potential loss.

Investors may choose to take options because the loss is limited to the price you pay for the token money. And in return, they gain the right to buy or sell stock at their desired price, so trading options benefit the investors.

Option Practicing Method

Stocks are purchased, and the investor sells call options on the same stock which they have purchased. The number of stock shares you have purchased should match the number of call options you have sold.

The investor purchase put options to gain equal shares after buying the stock shares. Married acts as an insurance policy in contrast to immediate losses call options with a particular strike price. At the same time, you will sell similar call options at a higher strike price.

An investor purchases an option with cash from outside while simultaneously works an out of the cash call choice for a similar stock.

The investor purchases a call option and a put choice simultaneously. The two alternatives ought to have a similar strike cost and expiry date.

The investor purchases the call option out of cash and the put choice simultaneously. They have a similar termination date; however, their strike cost is extraordinary. The expense of the information strike ought to be not exactly the expense of the call strike.

Features of the Options

Option contracts include typical terms and conditions for exchange-traded options. The following four elements for any exchange-traded option are specified in each contract option:

Underlying Security

Only a limited number of company shares referred to as the underlying securities, offer options traded on the ASX. The exchange determines these underlying securities based on their own set of guidelines. There is no control over the exchange-traded options issued with their shares by the companies themselves.

Contract Size

On the ASX, all contracts for exchange-traded options have a standard contract size of 100. Before that year, for all exchange-traded options contracts in Australia, the standard contract size was 1,000 shares. It aligns the ASX with the US markets, where the standard contract size is 100 shares per contract offer.

Expiration Date

Every option has a limited life depending on the expiry date of the option. The expiry date is the last day the contract can be exchanged (bought or sold), and all untrained options expire.

American style options can be exercised before the expiry date at any time. The bulk of options traded on the ASX are called in the American style. Nevertheless, there is another design type called choices for European style. It is only possible to practice European style choices on the expiry date and not before.

The expiry date of stock options is Thursday before the month's last Friday. Therefore, the expiry date is quoted as a month instead of a specific date. Options will be cited as having expiry dates set on the March, June, September, and December financial quarters, plus monthly expiry dates for the next three to six months, depending on the options category.

Strike Price

The exercise price or strike price is when the remaining stock price can be acquired or sold if the right is exercised. For all options listed on the ASX options market, it sets the strike prices. For each underlying security, there are several strike prices set for each expiry date option. As the market value of the underlying security increases, new strike orders will be released.

Premium

The premium alternative is the only part that the exchange does not standardize. The premium is the amount at which a buyer and seller buy and sells the contract.

The price of buying and selling shares on the stock exchange is dictated by the supply and demand powers. Buyers put in offers to buy the stock, and sellers put in bids to sell their stock, which decides the market price when they touch. For alternatives, this is not the case.

Option premiums are calculated by a mix of factors, including the underlying security's market value, the option's strike price, and the expiry period.

Option premiums (or prices) are quoted as "cents per share" overstocks. You need to subtract the "cents per share" by the number of shares protected by the option (usually 100) to determine the overall premium for a particular option. Therefore, a $1.50 swap traded offer will cost you $150.00 to purchase ($1.50 per share or 100 shares per contract). With the trading and exchange fees, you would also have your transaction fees on top of that.

CHAPTER 4:

Learning the Lingo

Options traders speak their language. It's not meant to confuse you, and it's just the natural process of creating a shorthand by which one trader can converse with another more easily and thoroughly.

Of course, it does make it difficult to plunge into the waters of options trading if you can't speak the language. It is a lot like trying to decipher road signs in a foreign country. It makes it hard to know the right direction—or even where you're standing right now.

We're going to take a look at the common terms you'll be dealing with as you enter the world of options trading before, we begin taking a deeper look at your strategies.

Don't worry about trying to learn the terms by rote. They will all become clear as you forge onward. This glossary will always be available to you so that you can check on meaning if you need to.

- **Strike price:** A price per share agreed upon before an option is traded. At that price, a stock may be bought or sold under the terms of your option contract. This price is also known as the "exercise price."

- **Bid/ask:** The latest price that a market maker has offered for an option is its "ask" price. In other words, it's what the seller is willing to accept for the trade. The latest amount that a buyer has offered for an option is the "bid" price.

- **Premium:** The premium is a per-share amount paid to the seller to procure an option. The seller will keep that premium whether the buyer exercises their right to buy or sell the stock at the deadline.

- **In-the-money:** Often shortened to ITM, that means that the stock price is above the strike price for a call or below the strike price for a put. In other words, it is now at the right price to be traded.

- **Out-of-the-money:** Often shortened to OTM, that means the current price is below the strike price for a call or above it for a put. Such an option is priced according to "time value."

- **At-the-money:** The strike price is equal to the current stock price.

- **Long:** In this context, "long" is used to imply ownership. Once you purchase a stock or option, you are "long" that item in your account.

- **Short:** If you sell an option or stock that you do not own, you are "short" that security in your account.

- **Exercise:** The option owner takes advantage of the right to buy or sell what they purchased with the option by "exercising" it.

- **Assigned:** When an owner of an option exercises it, the seller is "assigned" and must make good on the trade. In other words, the seller must fulfill their obligation to buy or sell.

- **Intrinsic value/time value:** The intrinsic value of an option refers to how much it is ITM. Most options also include time value, and that refers to how long is left until the option expires. That time has value because, during that time, the stock can still change in price.

- **Time decay:** Linked to time value, that term refers to the fact that, as time ticks on, the amount of time value slowly decreases. At the expiration date of an option contract, the contract has NO time value and is worth only its intrinsic value.

- **Index options/equity options:** Index options are settled by cash, whereas equity options involve trading stock. The main difference between those two options is that an index option usually cannot be exercised before the expiration date, while an equity option usually can.

- **Stop-loss order:** That is an order to sell either an option or a stock when it reaches a particular price. Its purpose is to set a point at which you, as the trader, would like to get out of your position. At that price, your stop order is activated as a market order. In other words, a market order looks for the best available price at that moment to close out your position.

Those are the most common terms you will hear used as you venture into the world of options trading. It's worth mentioning that, as you extend your understanding, you'll encounter more terms. However, the above terms are enough to help you understand your first trades.

CHAPTER 5:

Types of Trading Options

There is a wide range of types and styles of options accessible. This segment gives a picture of each kind just as some essential wording each option investors should be comfortable with.

Call Options

A call option gives the investor the right (not the commitment) to buy the fundamental stock, security, item, or other instruments, at a particular cost within the contract's time. The predefined cost is known as the strike cost. A speculator who is bullish on the stock, which means they anticipate that the stock should go up within a short time or inside the particular period, would buy a call option.

For instance, say Investor A thinks stock XYZ will post high income one month from now, and the stock will go higher. So, they buy a call option on the stock for $20. The option agreement determines that they can buy 100 portions of XYZ at a strike cost of $100 within the following sixty days. If the cost of the stock falls beneath $100, then they won't practice the option. The agreement will terminate uselessly, and they will have lost the $20 price tag.

In any case, if the cost of the stock transcends $100, state to $130, then they will practice the option, buy the stock for $100, and afterward, sell it at the higher market cost. They have now made a pleasant benefit.

Put Options

A put option is something contrary to a call option. It gives the owner the right (however, not the commitment) to sell the fundamental stock at a predetermined value (the strike cost) inside the predefined period. An investor who is bearish on the stock, which means they think the stock cost is going down, would buy a put option.

For instance, say Investor B thinks stock XYZ is overrated and will decrease in cost throughout the following sixty days. Then they buy a put option on the stock for $20. The agreement gives them the option to sell the stock for $120 within the following sixty days. If the stock transcends $120 per share, then they would not practice the option. It would lapse useless, and they have lost their underlying speculation. If rather the cost of the stock dips under $120, to state $90, then they would practice their entitlement to sell the offers at $120 and pocket the distinction as a profit.

Make a Profit Using Call and Put Options

There are various ways you can use call and put options. For instance, assume you believe that portions of US banks selling for $200 per share are undervalued and will go higher in the following couple of months. You need more money to buy at least 100 portions of stock, yet you might, in any case, want to bring in money from the ascent in the stock.

For this situation, you could buy a call option on the stock, which would cost just a small amount of the stock's cost. So, you buy the call option, and you presently reserve the option to buy 100 portions of the stock at $200 whenever in the following sixty days.

You may be thinking about buying the stock in the next sixty days for $200 per share if I don't have the money; the appropriate response is that you don't need to buy the stock to make a profit. If your impulses are right and the stock cost rises above $200, then your call option will turn out to be increasingly important. At the end of the day, as the stock value rises, the value of your option agreement likewise rises. You will have the option to sell the option agreement itself, rather than the stock, and make a benefit. The higher the value rises, the more your agreement will be worth.

This works a similar route for a put option, but you need the stock cost to fall in this situation. As the cost of the hidden security drops, the value of your put option will rise. The further the value falls, the more important is your option.

As should be obvious, by buying options, you can profit whether or not the stock is going up or down in cost.

Styles of Options

The past segments have reviewed the two essential sorts of options, calls, and puts. This segment will assist you in understanding the different styles of options accessible.

Most options you will buy will be categorized as one of two classifications: American or European. These are once in a while known as vanilla options. The principle distinction between the two is the point at which you can practice the option.

- **American options:** American options can be practiced whenever before the expiry date. Most options on stocks and value are of this sort. These are additionally the kind of agreements exchanged on fates trades.

- **European options:** European options must be practiced on the lapse date characterized in the agreement. These sorts of options are, for the most part, exchanged over the counter (OTC) advertisements.

The two options styles' values are determined marginally distinctively, and their termination dates are also unique. American options lapse the third Saturday of the month, while European options terminate the Friday before the third Saturday of the month.

Similitudes between the two incorporate the result and the strike cost. The result, either for calls or puts, is determined similarly for the two kinds. In like manner, the strike costs ordinarily are the equivalent.

Extraordinary Options

While the over two styles are the primary ones most investors will manage, there is an assortment of increasingly colorful option sorts to know about too:

- **Bermuda options:** Bermuda options are in the middle of American and European options. In this kind of option, you are permitted to practice them on numerous dates during the agreement time frame.

- **Barrier options:** Barrier options are not the same as the different sorts talked about so far in that all together for the option to result in the cost of the basic security must cross a specific level. They can be either be put or call options. There are four sorts of barrier options, which are plot beneath:
  - ○ **Down-and-out:** A Down-and-out barrier option gives the holder the privilege, however, not the commitment to buy (on account of a call) or sell (on account of a put) portions of a hidden resource at a foreordained strike cost since the cost of that advantage didn't go beneath a foreordained barrier during the option lifetime. That is, when the cost of the hidden resource falls underneath the barrier, the option is "took out" and no longer conveys any worth. Hence, the name out for the count.

- **Down-and-in:** A down-and-in option is something contrary to a done for barrier option. Down-and-in options possibly convey value if the fundamental resource's cost falls beneath the barrier during the option's lifetime. If the barrier is crossed, the holder of the down-and-in option has the option to buy (if it is a call) or sell (if it is a put) portions of the hidden resource at the foreordained strike cost on the termination date.

- **Up-and-out:** An up-and-out barrier option is like a done for barrier option, the main contrast being the arrangement of the barrier. Instead of being taken out by falling beneath the barrier cost, up-and-out options are taken out if the cost of the hidden resource transcends the foreordained barrier.

- **Up-and-in:** An up-and-in barrier option is like a down-and-in option; anyway, the barrier is set over the present cost of the hidden resource, and the option might be substantial if the cost of the basic resource arrives at the barrier before lapse.

- **Basket options:** A basket option, otherwise called a rainbow option, is an agreement wherein the worth depends on at least two basic resources. The option to practice the option is reliant on the costs of every fundamental resource.

- **Capped style options:** In this kind of agreement, the most extreme benefit is set up. Capped options contain an arrangement where the option is practiced consequently if the fundamental security arrives at a specific set up cost. These kinds of options offer the author of the option a most extreme sum that can be lost.

- **Compound options:** These are fundamental options to buy an option. Additionally, it is called split-expense options because the holder must compensate two premiums, one forthright and one if the option is worked out.

- **Lookback options:** This style of option supplies the holder of the option to either buy or sell the fundamental security at its top (on account of calls) or most reduced (on account of puts) cost over a predetermined period.

- **Asian options:** Asian options, otherwise called normal options, depend upon the mean (normal) cost of the fundamental security over a particular period.

- **Binary options:** Binary options have a payout that is either a fixed sum or nothing by any stretch of the imagination. There are two sorts: money or-nothing and resource or-nothing.

The holder will get a fixed measure of money in the primary kind if the option lapses in-the-money. In the advantage or-nothing assortment, the holder would get the value of the hidden security.

Otherwise called digital options, win big or bust options and fixed bring options back. The bit of leeway to this kind of option is that the potential return is a known sureness before the option is bought. Notwithstanding, once bought, they can't be sold before the lapse.

- **Forward start options:** Forward beginning options start with a vague strike value that will be resolved later on.

- **LEAPS:** LEAPS represents Long-Term Equity Anticipation Securities. LEAPS are equivalent to customary options except the more drawn out lapse dates. A LEAP can have a lapse date that is as long as three years away. The favorable position to this kind of option is there is much more opportunity for the basic stock, and along these lines option, to move toward the path you need it to.

- **Index options:** Notwithstanding buying options on singular protections, you can likewise buy options on a stock list.

  These can be engaging even though they give an introduction to a whole gathering of stocks. List options are adaptable and can fit both moderate and theoretical investors' systems during both a bull and a bear showcase. Most file options are European style options.

CHAPTER 6:

Options Pricing

Another useful aspect of options trading that you need to be familiar with is pricing options. The option price is also known as the option premium and consists of two distinct components. These are the intrinsic value and extrinsic value. The put-call parity principle governs both.

How to Price Options?

Another factor that you need to be conversant with is how to price an option. You must be able to price options correctly and accurately so that you do not incur unnecessary losses. The first step in pricing options is to understand all the elements that are involved.

The pricing process is a science and not an art. Once you master this science, you will be able to price options quite easily. Numerous external factors determine options prices. However, 90% of the time, volatility, stock price, and time till expiration are influenced by volatility.

Factors to Consider

Stock Price

When pricing options, the first place to begin is the market price of the underlying security. The security could be an index, a stock, or even ETF (electronically traded fund). This price is the predominant factor in determining the price of a stock.

Imagine Apple's stock trading at $500. The company then introduces a new gadget in the market. This new product is even greater than current gadgets like the iPhone. The shares then gain value and tend towards $550. In such an instance, many shareholders will want to secure exclusive rights to buy the shares at $520. As the price of the shares goes up, so do the call prices.

Time

Options are a factor of time. This means that they are wasting assets. In other words, their benefits are limited within a certain stipulated period. It may be three months or six months. As an option approaches its expiration date, there is less time to benefit from it. As such, its value decreases proportionately. You must always factor in time when pricing options.

Bid and Ask Price

Another crucial factor that plays an important part in option pricing is the bid or ask price. Regardless of whether it is a call or put, each option always has a bid and ask price.

When buying options, you will purchase at the asking price or very close to it and sell on the bid or near it. For instance, if you are looking at September 75 calls and notice prices like $9.60 x $9.90, then the asking price you'd be purchasing is $9.90 while the selling price on this option has its lower margins at $9.60. The difference between these two prices is that the asking price and bid price is known as the spread. If the spread is very tight, then it means that the stock is very liquid.

Volatility

Yet another important factor that determines the price of an option is its volatility. Volatility is the most crucial factor in the stock price. Any options based on very long-term stable stocks will be predictably priced compared to options whose stocks have hugely volatile charts. Apart from past performance, implied volatility is also crucial, so all these factors are considered when pricing a stock.

Other Factors Influencing Prices of Options

In both puts and calls, the market maker or investor receives a premium. The premium is the fee of acquiring an option. Here are some of the factors that affect the price of an option:

Probability

The chance that an option will end up in-the-money is the main aspect influencing an option's worth.

The closer the probability that the underlying asset will end up in-the-money gets to 100%, the greater the option's worth becomes; the further away the probability that the underlying asset will finish in-the-money gets from 100%, the lower the value of the option. As a trader, you have to sharpen your analytical skills and determine whether an option is worthy of the premium it demands.

Interest Rates

You must note that rates of interest have a slight effect on the value of an option. When the rates of interest increase, the call's worth will go up, and the put option will go down. The adjustments in the premiums are triggered by the costs of owning the underlying assets. When a trader acquires an options contract, the extra cash can attract interest. A high interest translates into bigger earnings. Therefore, traders are willing to pay higher premiums to own call options.

Dividends

When a trader fails to receive their dividend, the stock will go down by that amount. A dividends increment causes a rise in the value of both calls and puts.

Natural Logarithm

The Black-Scholes calculation of premiums utilizes the natural logarithm. The changes in the price of underlying assets are proportional to the price of the underlying.

Normal Distribution

The normal probability distribution is used in the calculation of an options price. In the Black-Scholes model, price movement is understood to be distributed normally. Small movements have a high probability, whereas large movements have low probability.

News

It seems that financial news plays a critical role in driving the whole derivatives markets. Although chances of it happening are rare, influential finance journalists could drive a plan that could trigger oscillations in the price of options contracts. But the real captains of the industry are the brokers and market makers. These people who are in charge of brokerages and market-making corporations have the power to influence the course of the derivatives market. When they appear on the news, traders and investors hang on their every word, and traders could go on a spree of buying or selling, which affects the value of options.

Crowd Psychology

If there's a sector that asks for mental maturity and discipline, it's the derivatives market. You have to have a plan and know when to take action instead of guessing your way around. But people are still people. It's so easy to get distracted by the trends and lose sight of your trading strategy. For instance, if a certain clique of traders reaps sudden profits, everyone runs into their niche in the hope of reaping quick benefits, thus driving the premium of the option up.

Price of the Underlying Asset

While they often will not move at the same speed or for the same amounts, an option will always follow the lead of its underlying asset. As such, you can always expect the price of related calls to increase along with rising asset prices, while puts will always decrease and vice versa.

Time Value

The amount of time that an option has until it expires is directly related to how likely that same option will ultimately end in a profit greater than the intrinsic value before things are said and done. To determine the amount of time value that the option you are considering offers currently, you will want to find the option's current price and subtract from it the amount of intrinsic value that the same option currently has. It is common for options to hold onto 70% of their total value, or more, during the first half of their life before losing value much more rapidly after that point. You also have to remember that time value can change dramatically based on the volatility of the underlying asset both in the moment and based on its expectations in the future. As a general rule, the lower the time value, the more stable the option will be.

Intrinsic Value

The amount of value that an option will hold onto, even at the end of its lifespan, is known as the intrinsic value. When working with a call option, you can find the intrinsic value by taking the current price of the underlying asset and dividing that by the difference between the strike price and the current price.

When it comes to finding the intrinsic value of a put option, the process is mostly the same; to start, you subtract the amount the underlying asset is currently worth from its strike price before dividing that number by the current stock price.

This equation's results will provide you with a clearer idea of the type of advantage that choosing to exercise the option at the moment would provide you with. It can also be the minimum that the option will ever be worth, even at the moment of its expiration.

CHAPTER 7:

Benefits of Options Trading

There are a few of the primary benefits of trading in options and why you may consider purchasing or offering options as a part of your total trading method. We will also learn the significant dangers in buying and providing options, remembering that the risks included in options are substantially different for buyers of options than the risks for sellers of options.

When purchasing options, you invest in an asset with no real worth, which may be worthless within a few months. As you will quickly find, there are numerous benefits of trading options that can be used in a wide variety of methods.

We will now describe a few of the main advantages of options. These are extended attributes that apply to options. As we talk about the types of options in more detail and the methods used for each kind of option, you will see the benefits (and drawbacks) of trading options.

A benefit to a seller will typically equate to a downside to the buyer and vice versa. The factor this operates in the marketplace is, the reason or strategy used by the seller is different from the idea the purchaser has participated in the agreement.

When evaluating the benefits of using options, you likewise need to think about the risks associated with your particular options method.

Danger Management

Options provide financiers with the ability to manage danger within their portfolio. Options can provide a financier with a hedge versus falls in the price of their present stock holdings. It can effectively allow a financier to lock in some profits on their holding without physically selling their shares.

This can be useful when an investor wishes to maintain their shares for a longer-term or does not want to understand a capital gain by offering their investment at the current time.

Purchasing a put option allows you to buy the right to sell your present shares at an advantageous price if you anticipate a fall in the cost of those shares before the expiry date of the option. The investors are allowed to gain on the put options that will offset a loss on the physical shares on the occasion that the stocks do fall in value.

You own 3000 shares in a stock presently trading at $10.50. You want to secure some revenue at this price as you feel that the price will fall in the brief term. To use this strategy, you purchase 30 put option agreements with a strike cost of $10.50. This costs you to buy $0.20 per share in each agreement (with 100 shares in each transaction).

This purchase allows you to offer 3000 shares at $10.50 whenever before the option's expiry date. Your put option value will increase by a similar quantity (less any ended time worth) if the stock rate subsequently falls. Thus, you are safeguarding yourself against a fall in the price of your stock. A fall in the worth of your stock will be balanced by a rise in your options' value.

If the stock cost stays at or above $10.50, then you would either not exercise your options or sell your option close to the expiration date (although it would deserve very little).

If the stock rate does fall to, state, $9.50, then the worth of your put options would increase by $1.00 (less any expired time worth). You could then offer these options for approximately $1.00 and realize earnings of $3000.00. This will balance out the fall in worth of your shareholding of a similar amount. Effectively, you have paid $600.00 for your options to defend you against the fall in the stock position price.

Speculation

The capability to trade online and the listing of options on the ASX make it very simple to purchase and offer options. The options trading makes it possible for traders to buy an option contract with the intent of selling the options before the expiration date for a revenue. The traders may have expectations of an increase in the option (due to a change in the underlying security cost). And no objective of ever exercising the option if your option has intrinsic value.

The value of your options will change much in line with the change in worth of the underlying stock. You will also see a fall in quality that is unrelated to any change in worth of the hidden security but is due to a fall in the option's time value as it nears expiry.

How options move with changes in the value of the underlying stock. These movements are for options that have an intrinsic worth in their premium.

As a speculator, you can acquire call options if you expect the underlying security rate to increase. As the security rate's underlying price rises, your options' intrinsic value will increase by a similar amount if you anticipate the underlying security rate to fall. Your method may be to buy put options as the price of the underlying security drops. The intrinsic options' value will increase by a similar amount. To produce a profit, you need the worth of the underlying security to move in your favor before the expiry date, and you would need to offer your option on or before the expiration date.

When purchasing and after offering American style stock options to generate short-term revenue, you need to ensure you sell your options before the expiry date. This requires the cost of the underlying stock to move in your favor before the expiry date.

Leverage

Leverage can produce the same return level from a prospective financial investment; however, utilizing a smaller sized initial expense. If you owned the real shares, purchasing a call option with intrinsic value exposes you to a comparable gain or loss that you would attain. The cost of a fraction of the price options of the underlying stock. This permits you to benefit from changes in the stock's value without paying the capital's full fee.

Leverage does come with a new threat; the gains are amplified through the usage, so too are any losses. Some examples show how force can create a more significant portion of return than can direct financial investment.

Your returned percentage can be magnified as a result of the leverage achieved through the usage of options. It is necessary to note that your losses can be equally magnified in some circumstances. Nevertheless, your loss will always be limited to the premium you spent on the opportunity when purchasing options.

Idea

When speculating using options, you need to represent the fall in time worth of your option and your ideal costs when assessing your trading opportunity.

Diversification

The use of options can offer you the opportunity to benefit from the motion in a stock rate at a portion of the stock price. This permits you to construct a varied portfolio for a lower preliminary expense. This comes at a cost as your options include a value for the time of expiry, which will decrease to no over the option's life.

Income Generation

When selling an option, you get an advance premium from the purchaser of your option. The premium kept, whether or not the option has worked out. This premium can produce an income stream if carefully selected options are sold on a systematic basis. The seller maintains the premium and has no further commitment if the options are not exercised.

There are several methods based on offering options to generate premium income. The goal is to sell options that are not likely to be worked out or purchase back (closeout) your options before the expiration date if there is a danger they will be exercised.

CHAPTER 8:

Disadvantages of Options Trading

Options have many advantages, but just like any other investment, they have disadvantages too. The investor must understand both sides of the coin, the good and the bad, before committing their resources to options trading. Following are some of the shortfalls of options trading (The advantages and disadvantages of options, n.d.):

Tax

Except for extremely rare instances, all your gains are taxed as income. This is the same as taxing your income because the tax rates levied upon your gains are just as high. One clever way investors can step around the taxation issue is to utilize their tax-deferred accounts such as the IRA. Sadly, not everyone has ownership of a tax-deferred account. The tax can reduce the amount of money you take home, but considering the high earning potential, options are still profitable.

Commissions

In comparison to stock investing, commissions for options are significantly higher. For most active traders, their annual commissions usually exceed 30% of the total amount you invested. To guard yourself against paying exorbitant commissions, never sign up with a broker without being clear.

Whenever you receive a newsletter, quickly check to see the commission details. Options trades will cost you more in commission for every dollar that you put down. The commissions may even be more for spreads that require you to pay commissions for both sides. A trader should be careful about the broker that they choose to work with. For instance, if you're a beginner, you should stick to brokers who cater to beginners.

Time Value Decay

In stock trading, you can purchase long-term stocks that can take decades to mature. But options contracts come with an expiration date. You can't stop the process of expiring. Also, the option's position relative to expiration dates affects the premium that you will pay to acquire the option. The more the options get closer to the expiration date, the more the rate of time value decay increases. Therefore, monitor your open positions so that your options don't expire worthlessly.

Uncertainty of Gains

Investors try to minimize risk by examining the risk profile graphs. This shows them the projected gains or losses at the next expiration of options contracts. In as much as these graphs are helpful, especially when placing the initial position, they still cannot guarantee you a profit. It can be hard to project the gains from an options trade. Sometimes, after the expiration of options contracts, the expected gains are not generated. But there are other times when, at the expiration of options contracts, the earnings exceed the projected gains. In that sense, your gains or losses become somewhat uncertain—terrible for individuals who loathe uncertainty.

Loss of Investment

The extent of your losses depends in large measure on your investment strategy. If you put together a strategy aimed at the highest possible returns, the risk is considerably higher. During the contract's lifetime, the underlying's price can depreciate, and at expiration, you would not exercise your option. You will only lose the premium; a stock trader would lose their shares.

Regulation

One of the things that bother traders and investors is the regulations imposed by governing bodies. The OCC, Securities, and Exchange Commission (SEC), or even The Court, has the power to impose restrictions on exercising various options. Although it rarely happens, it is still enough of a concern that it can make traders think again before putting down their resources into acquiring options contracts. You should always perform your due diligence over the underlying assets you intend to take options contracts for. If the assets are at the center of legal battles, you might want to take a pass.

Lower Liquidity

A lot of individual stock options don't have much volume. If it is not among the most popular stocks or indexes, the option you're trading is likely to be low volume because each stock will have a different strike price and expiration. Remember that liquidity issue only becomes a huge factor if the trades are big money. In the case of a small trader who purchases around ten options contracts, liquidity is never an issue.

Complicated

It's not beginners alone who can get overwhelmed in the world of options trading. Some professional traders seem to think that they understand options trading when they don't. To understand options trading, you have to dedicate a significant amount of time to study all the aspects of this field. As a beginner, the worst mistake you can commit is to sign up with a broker that caters to professional traders. You have to look for a broker that caters to beginners so that you could utilize their educational resources. There's so much to learn before anyone could become proficient in options trading.

Leverage

When it comes to options trading, leverage is a double-edged sword. On the one hand, it can minimize the risk surrounding an underlying, and on the other hand, it can affect the performance of the asset's market value. When an underlying price is affected negatively, it means that your earning potential is constrained. Leverage is most dangerous when you're selling naked options or entering into unlimited-risk strategies. Options trading affords investors many trading tools. The tools can make or break you. It is upon the investor to use these trading tools for their benefit.

The biggest step an investor can take for success in options trading is acquiring the requisite knowledge. Guesswork is bound to get you into major losses.

CHAPTER 9:

Tips for Getting Started on Options Trading

Although it seems complex and can include a wide range of strategic approaches, it's relatively easy to start trading options.

You need a broker, and you will need to compare fees and account minimums so that you can choose one that is affordable and meets your investment style.

From there, it's time to develop your strategy for trading options. Like most investment options, trading strategies is dependent on your personal goals and tolerance for risk and can range from simple to complex.

Create a Brokerage Account

If you're interested in trading options, you'll need to open a brokerage to access your transactions—this can be done online or through a standard broker account. Be sure you fully grasp what's involved in creating a brokerage account before you do that.

Compare the options trading commissions between different brokerages. Some firms do not even offer commissions on trading options.

Carry out some research online and read the reviews of brokerage firms that are on your shortlist. Get knowledge from the mistakes of other people so you won't have to repeat them.

Observe for scam trading platforms and sites. Always thoroughly research the platform before you deposit any money. Avoid any platform with negative reviews or possible fraud reported.

A cash account will only permit the purchase of options to create a position. If you desire to sell an option to set up an account without the underlying asset, you will need a margin account.

If you want to trade online, make sure that your online brokerage accepts secure payment forms, like a secure credit card payment gateway or a third-party payment service such as PayPal, Payoneer, Skrill, Bitcoin, etc.

Get Approval to Trade Options

You will need approval from your brokerage before you start buying and selling options. Brokerage firms handling an account set limits based on experience and money in the account, and every firm has its own criteria to ensure that the customer knows what they are doing. You can't write a covered call without an options account. Brokerage firms want to make sure before trading that customers have a full understanding of the risks.

Covered call writing means selling the right to purchase your stock at a strike price during the option duration. The buyer has the right to do so, not the seller. The stock must be in the brokerage account and cannot be sold or exchanged while the call is pending.

Understanding Technical Analysis

Options are typically short-term investments, so you will be searching for price movements of the optioned security to make a healthy return soon. To accurately forecast these price fluctuations, you would need to grasp the fundamentals of the technical analysis.

Learn about the level of support and resistance. These are points where the stock hardly ever decreases below (support) or increases above (resistance). Support is the level at which significant security purchases have historically occurred. Resistance is the price level, where significant security sales have occurred in the past.

Understand the significance of the volume. If a stock changes towards a specific direction with a lot of volume behind it, it typically means a strong trend and can be a money-making opportunity.

Understand the patterns of the chart. History usually repeats itself, even in the case of stock prices. There are common trends that you can look for in stock price fluctuations that can show where the price is going.

Learn more about moving averages. The same case is when the stock price is above or below the common moving average of the prices. A thirty-day moving average is perceived to be more accurate than a ten-day moving average.

Start With "Paper Trading"

Resist every temptation to risk hard-earned money with a technique you've just learned.

Instead, go for paper trading or practice. Make use of a spreadsheet or a practice trading software to enter "pretend" trades. Then review your returns for at least a few months. If you make a decent return, work your way to real trading slowly.

Paper trading is different from real trading, as there is no mental pressure or commissions involved. It's a good idea to learn mechanics, but it's not a predictor of actual results. Real options trading is a very high risk, which can result in substantial losses for the investor. You can only trade with money that you can afford to lose.

Use the Limit Orders

Avoid having to pay market prices for options, as the execution price can be higher than expected. Instead, state your price with limit orders and maximize your return.

Reassess Your Strategy regularly

Determine if there is anything that can be done to enhance your return. Learn from your mistakes but repeat your effective strategies as well. And maintain a focused strategy; traders concentrate on a few positions, not on diversification. You should have not more than 10% of your investment portfolio in options.

You Can Join a Forum of Traders of Like Minds Online

If you're experimenting with advanced trading options strategies, you'll discover that a vital source of information (and help, after a few tough losses) is an online trading platform. Locate a forum to enable you to learn from the successes and other failures.

Think of Other Strategies for Trading Options

After you have made some successful trades, you can get cleared for more advanced options trading strategies. However, start trading on paper as well. This will make it much simpler for you to carry them out in real trading.

One such strategy is the "straddle," which includes trading on both sides of the market, purchasing a put and a call option with the same strike price and date of maturation so that you restrict your exposure. This strategy is most successful when the market moves up and down rather than in a single direction. There is also a risk that only one side will be exercisable.

A related strategy is the "strip." The strip is like a straddle but is actually a "bearish" strategy with twice the downward price movement's earning power. It is comparable to the straddle in its implementation, but with twice as many options purchased on the downside (put options).

Know More About the Greeks

Once you've perfected simple options trading and choose to move on to more advanced options trading, you will have to learn about the Greeks. These are measuring that traders use to maximize their returns.

CHAPTER 10:

Options Sellers

Selling options is a strategy that is used to generate regular income. Selling options is a little simpler but carries a higher risk.

Review of Selling Covered Calls

If you have 100 or more shares of a particular stock, you can sell covered calls against your shares. This is a usual strategy used by people to earn money off their shares, but you always face the risk that your shares will be called away if the option is exercised. A strategy that can be used is to sell out-of-the-money calls when you don't expect the share price to rise to the call option's strike price over the lifetime of the contract.

For example, Facebook is trading at $190.25 a share. You can sell a $210 call for $0.64, so for all 100 shares, one option contract would net you $64. This is for an expiration date of thirty days. Or you could take a higher level of risk and sell a $195 call for $4.05, which would give you a premium of $405 per option contract. If you had 500 shares, then you'd receive $2,025 in premiums. Not a bad passive income and all you have to do is hope that the share price stays below the strike price.

If the share price closes in on the strike price, then you will be faced with a dilemma—risk having the option exercised if the share price rises above the strike price, or you can buy back the option and cut into your profits.

With a few days left to expiration, the option you sold may be worth $2.05, so you could buy back the five options you sold, and you'd reduce your net profit to $1,000.

You could go further out, even selling LEAPS. In that case, the premium paid is much larger. A Facebook LEAP with a $195 call that expires in eighteen months has a premium of $30.58, so selling five contracts for your 500 shares could bring in an income of $15,290. Of course, there is a higher risk that the share price will rise above the strike price over eighteen months than there is over the short term.

The one principle to keep in mind selling covered calls is that you could lose your shares if the option is exercised. You should select a strike price that is of a higher amount than what you had paid for the shares. If you are forced to sell the shares, you are not taking a loss doing so. That can make losing the shares easier to deal with. So if we had purchased our shares at $200 a share, we would not select a $195 strike price because that represents a potential loss, which would be given by the price we paid for the shares minus the strike price and then less the premium aid, in this case, $200 - $195 - $4.05 so we'd end up losing $0.95 on the trade. If you had purchased the shares at a lower price, say $190 a share, then the $195 strike would make sense since if the stock price rose and the shares were called away, we'd still profit by selling the shares.

Protected puts are the put version of a covered call. The risk with a protected put is that the shares will be "put to you," and you will have to buy the shares, so you will be required to have enough capital in your account to cover the purchase.

Of course, the trick to selling options is to pick a strike price where you think the option will expire worthlessly. There is the risk that you are wrong, but if you think the share price will rise for Facebook, to use an example, you could sell a protected $190 put for $4.95, earning $495 per contract. If the share price rises, the options will expire worthlessly, and you would keep the premium and profit from the deal.

Selling Naked Puts

It is a popular strategy for traders that are given level 4 status. If you can get this level from your broker, you can consider this possibly profitable strategy. Of course, the key is choosing the right strike price.

When a put is "naked," that means it isn't backed by anything. However, you are still required by law to fulfill your obligations should the option be exercised, but one way that traders avoid this problem is by buying the options back if there is a chance they would be exercised. The time value may work in your favor, which will make the options cheaper and so you can buy them back and still profit.

Another consideration is to choose a relatively low implied volatility, which reduces the chances that the stock will move much over the lifetime of the option. But that is a trade-off as well, as implied volatility that is a few points higher can have a large increase in the premium received for selling the option.

Consider IBM. The stock price is at $139.20, but you could sell a thirty-day $135 put for $2.44, or $244. You could even sell in-the-money puts.

A $145 put would sell for $748. If you sold five contracts, that would be a thirty-day income of $3,640.

Selling in-the-money puts could be risky but beneficial if it was believed that IBM shares were set to rise in price. When the price rises above the strike price, then the options will expire worthlessly.

Selling LEAPS, while it carries higher risk since a long time to expiration gives a higher chance that the option will move in the amount, also allow you to sell at high premiums. A $130 put for IBM expiring in eighteen months would sell for $13.20, so selling five contracts would give you a premium of $6,600. Bid-Ask spreads can be large for LEAPS, and the volume is probably small. For this particular option, we find that the bid-ask spread is about 80 cents, which isn't too bad, meaning selling it might not be that difficult. Daily volume is small at 10, but the open interest is 1,282. Experienced traders often recommend an open interest of 500 or higher since that indicates enough people are buying the contracts.

The risk with naked puts is that you will be forced to buy the shares. Again, if it looks like that might turn out to be the case, you can buy the contracts back. Selling OTM options that expire in the near term can leave you in a better position since the options will probably expire worthlessly, and you will be able to keep the premium without having to buy back the options. If you have to buy the shares, the loss would be the share price minus the market price. But of course, you'd have to get the capital to buy the shares as well.

So, if you sold a put option on IBM with a strike price of $138 expiring in six weeks, it would sell for $3.70. If the share price dropped to $136, you'd have to use cash to buy the shares at $138 and possibly lose $2 a share by selling them—or you could keep them and wait for the price to go back up. Your loss would be offset by the premium, so your break-even point is the amount of the strike price less premium paid.

Selling Naked Calls

You can also sell naked calls. This means that you sell call options without owning the shares of stock. The risk that the option will be exercised means that you would have to buy the shares at a higher market price and then sell them at the lower strike price. So, the key here would be to sell out-of-the-money calls at strike prices that you doubt the stock will reach over the option's lifetime. The same strategies can be used, and if it looks like the share price is rising, you can buy the options back to avoid being assigned.

Looking at IBM, some modest out-of-the-money call options thirty days to expiration have good prices. A $141 call, which is almost $2 out-of-the-money, is $3.55, so selling one contract would give you $355.

Suppose that stock was trading at $195 a share. You could sell a call with a forty-five-day expiration with a strike price of $200 for $4.46, or $446. If we find that the share price has risen to $197 with ten days to expiration, the calls would now be priced at $1.88, or $188. So, you could buy them back and still have a profit of $258 per contract, avoiding the risk that you would be assigned if the share price kept rising.

Of course, at $3 out-of-the-money, you might wait. When the price of the share rises to $199 with seven days left, the calls would be $218, so you'd be cutting a little more into your profits. But if it dropped $1 the following day, then the call option would only be worth $1.58.

Remember, when you sell options, you make money on the time premium. Or put another way, time decay is your friend. Out-of-the-money, options lose value rapidly as the expiration date approaches.

The biggest risk with selling naked call options if you can't buy them back is to buy stocks at a high price and then selling them at a loss to honor your obligations. Supposed that a stock is trading at $95 a share, and you sell a call option that has a $100 strike price. If the stock breaks out and, say, rises to $130 a share, someone might exercise the option. Since you sold the call naked, you'd be forced to buy the shares at $130 and sell them at the $100 strike price, losing $30 a share, which would be partially offset by the premium, which might be around $1 per share.

So, selling naked calls can be profitable but carries a lot of risks as well. The key to selling naked calls successfully is picking the right strike price and choosing a stock that you don't believe will have price movements that are large enough to cause the option to be in-the-money.

Broker May Force Sale

Note that most brokerages may automatically exercise options that expire in-the-money. So, you will not want to let an option expire in-the-money unless you are prepared to buy or sell the shares as required.

CHAPTER 11:

Popular Options Strategies

When you understand the fundamentals of trading options, you can get things going. You should have a business plan if it relates to options trading strategies. Just what will help you decide in your trading plan what kind of strategy to introduce. You will choose to create a strategy that will lead you to achieve your goals, depending on your trading plan.

Trading options stand the chance of failing. Recognizing what you do, however, is, by far, an essential factor. It will always be a threat to trade and invest; you need to have a good outlook on what you are doing. Establishing a successful trading strategy and then implementing a series of strategies to allow you to achieve it is the secret to a consistent and significant edge in trading options.

Traders often get started with trading options with little or no knowledge of the option strategies available. There are several solutions to alternatives that both minimize risk and optimize return. With just a little work, investors can learn to take advantage of the flexibility and flexibility that stock options can offer.

Here we will list some trading options strategies that every trader needs to know to manipulate the market:

Covered Call

A covered call translates as a financial operation where the owner selling call options holds an equal number of the corresponding security. To do this, a trader keeping a long position through an asset sells call options to create a revenue stream on the same investment. The investor's long position in the commodity is "cover," as it means that if the buyer wishes to utilize the call option, the seller will transfer the shares. It is regarded as a "buy-write" trade if the investor purchases the stock at one time and writes call options on that stock.

- A covered call would be a common options technique used in the pattern of options premiums to make profits.

- A trader maintaining a long position through investment then writes call options on the same investment to conduct a covered call.

- Many who wish to retain the underlying asset for a long time are often using covered calls but do not anticipate a substantial price rise in the short future.

- For a trader who thinks the associated price will not change much through the near-term, this approach is perfect.

Covered calls are often a balanced strategy, implying that the investor expects a small rise or decline in the corresponding stock price for the written call contract duration. This approach is often used when a trader has an impartial short-term perception of the commodity and, for this purpose, keeps the asset longer and also has a short position through the option to earn revenue from the premium at the same time.

A covered call acts as short-term leverage on a prolonged position and enables investors to gain revenue for selling the option through the premium obtained. The investor, though, revokes stock profits if the price rises above the option's purchase price. If the trader wants to exercise the option, they are also obliged to offer 100 shares at the market price (for every contract written).

Married Put

An investor buys a share, such as company shares, in a married put approach, and concurrently buys options for an equal amount of stocks. The put option owner is entitled to offer the stocks at the strike rate, and the value of each agreement is 100 shares.

When maintaining a portfolio, an investor can utilize such a strategy to preserve their market risk. This solution operates comparably to an insurance plan; if the stock price drops sharply, it sets a price floor.

A married put is a term referring to an options trading approach in which an investor buys an at-the-money (ATM) put option on the very same share, maintaining a long position in such a product, to hedge against a decline in the stock's price.

A married put is also called a long synthetic call since it has the same pattern of benefit. The method is similar to purchasing a standard call option (without any of the underlying assets) since the same dynamic applies to both: restricted loss and infinite benefit potential.

Bull Call Spread

An investor concurrently buys calls at a particular strike price in a bull call spread technique while still offering the very same number of calls at a higher price. There will be the same expiry date and underlying security for both call options. Whenever a trader is optimistic about the financial commodity, this form of spread strategy is mostly used and projects a modest increase in the asset values. Using this method, the investor can reduce its trade advantage while also diminishing premiums spent (compared to buying a naked call option outright).

Bear Put Spread

Another type of vertical spread is the bear-put spread approach. Concurrently, in this technique, the investor buys put options at a particular strike price and sells the same volume of puts at a lower price. For the same financial commodity, all options are acquired to have the same expiry date. This technique can be used when the investor has a bearish feeling regarding the financial commodity and anticipates its price to decrease. The strategy generates both restricted losses and constrained gains.

Protective Collar

By buying an out-of-the-money (OTM) put option and concurrently selling an out-of-the-money (OTM) call option, a protective collar approach is carried out. The corresponding asset, as well as the date of expiry, must be similar. Sometimes after a long position throughout a stock has seen considerable returns, this technique is also used by traders. As the long put makes it easier to lock in the future sale price, investors also have risk security. The trade-off, though, is that they will be forced to sell securities at a premium cost, leaving aside the prospect of more gain.

Straddles

A straddle is a neutral option technique involving the mutual acquisition of both a call option and a put option with much the same market price and the same expiry date for the underlying stock when the value of the security increases or drops from the market price by a sum more significant than the premium charge's cumulative value. An investor will benefit from such a long straddle as much as the value of the underlying product shifts very abruptly; the profit potential is practically limitless.

A straddle may offer two important clues to an investor about what the market for options feels about some inventory. The first is the uncertainty predicted from the protection by the sector. The second is the stock's estimated trading scope by the date of maturity.

A strategy of extended straddle options happens when an investor buys a call simultaneously and puts an option along with the same asset class with the same purchase price and expiry date. A trader can also use this technique if they assume that the underlying stock's value will move dramatically out of a particular range, but they are not sure which path the transfer will take. This method allows the trader, ideally, to have the potential for limitless profits.

Strangles

A strangle is a technique of options wherein the investor owns a place with varying strike rates, with almost the same expiry date and financial instrument, in both a put and a call option. If you assume the underlying asset will undergo a significant price action in the immediate future but are not sure of the course, a stranglehold is an excellent approach. It is, nevertheless, lucrative primarily if the investment swings in price dramatically.

A strangle is closely related to a straddle, except at varying strike rates, uses alternatives, whereas a straddle utilizes a call and places it at a similar strike price.

The trader purchases an OTM put and an OTM call option concurrently in a long strangle.

The call option's market rate seems to be greater than the existing selling price of the associated asset, whereas the put has a lesser market price than the asset's selling price. As when the call option has potentially infinite potential if the asset value increases in value, this strategy has huge benefit prospects. In contrast, the put option will generate income if the asset value falls. The transaction risk is restricted to the premium charged for the options.

Long Call Butterfly Spread

The traditional approaches required the integration of two specific positions or agreements. An investor can mix both a bear spread strategy and a bull spread strategy within a long butterfly spread utilizing call options. There are three different strike rates they can all use. All options are from similar underlying stock and maturity dates.

For instance, by buying one in-the-money (ITM) call option at a lower rate while still offering two at-the-money (ATM) call options as well as purchasing one out-of-the-money (OTM) call option, a long butterfly spread can be established. Relatively similar wing dimensions would be available for a consistent butterfly spread. This instance is termed a "call fly" and a cumulative debit result from it. When they assume that the stocks will not change much until expiry, a trader will move into a long butterfly call spread.

Iron Condor

The investor concurrently owns a bear call spread and a bull put spread within the iron condor approach. By offering one out-of-the-money (OTM) put and purchasing one out-of-the-money (OTM) put off a lesser strike-a-bull put spread and writing one out-of-the-money (OTM) call and purchasing one out-of-the-money (OTM) call of a greater strike-a bear call spread, the iron condor is established. Both options would be on the same asset class and have the same expiry date. The call and put sides usually have the very same spread diameter. This investment thesis provides a net profit framework and is structured to fully leverage a low-volatility stock. Many investors use this technique for its expected high likelihood of receiving a small amount of fee.

Iron Butterfly

An investor will write an at-the-money (ATM) put in the iron butterfly strategy and purchase an out-of-the-money (OTM) put. They would also transfer an at-the-money (ATM) call at the very same time and purchase an out-of-the-money (OTM) call. Both options would be on the same asset class and have the same expiry date. Although this method is close to a butterfly spread, it makes use of both puts and calls.

This approach effectively incorporates the sale of an at-the-money (ATM) straddle and the purchase of defensive "wings." The development can also be interpreted as two spreads. In both spreads, it is customary to get the same dimension. The long, infinite downside is covered by the out-of-the-money (OTM) call.

The long out-of-the-money (OTM) put protects against the disadvantages. Based on the price levels of the options utilized, benefits, and losses, both are limited to a particular range. Investors like this method for the revenue it produces and the greater possibility of a small benefit from a non-volatile portfolio.

CHAPTER 12:

Practical Example

We will talk about essential trading habits and give you examples of excellent option trading strategies. Remember this information can be used to decide to take part in any trading.

The medium and long-term investment is ideal for those who want to build capital or diversify and enhance savings over time naturally and at reduced costs. Given their versatility, ETFs can be used in different medium and long-term investment strategies. They can support or replace traditional instruments, thus allowing them to achieve the set objective. Currently, the range of ETFs is so diverse that any FCI can be replicated (at a much higher cost)

A strategy to invest its capital in the medium to long term is to resort to investment funds, whose popularity has grown progressively over the last twenty years. One of the funds' main characteristics is allowing the underwriter to enter the market with modest capital and obtain professional management that will allow them to obtain positive results over time, with moderate risk. Investment funds should favor more active management, even if this does not always happen.

In addition to weighing on their final return, they are the highest management costs to which the same funds are subject. Their impact is felt particularly in times of slowdown or stagnation of the market. In light of this situation, the investor could find it convenient to substitute the investment in funds with that of ETFs that aim to follow the evolution of its benchmark index carefully while offering the maximum possible transparency.

In advance, it cannot be said whether it is better to invest in funds or ETF; to make this choice, you have to decide if you want the manager to move away from the benchmark (and from which benchmark): this possibility is called "active risk." Active risk is not necessarily bad because some managers are better than others. Still, in reality, they are few, and, not always, you can find them. If you decide to move away from the underlying risk, you must be convinced that:

- Good managers exist.

- That they can do better than their benchmark.

- Above all, be able to find them.

If you think you can complete each of the three phases, it is appropriate to rely on active funds. Otherwise, ETFs are preferred because they cost less and carry precisely where you decided to go without additional surprises.

The techniques for choosing the ETF that best suits your investment strategies are different; an interesting methodology is applied to sector rotation.

The market is made up of different equity sectors, corresponding to the different economic sectors and their continuous alternation from the origin to the expansion and contraction phases. Thus, the moments in which all the economic sectors grow or decrease simultaneously are quite rare. The concept of sector rotation is useful to identify, on the one hand, the stage of maturity of the current primary trend and, on the other, to select those sectors that have a growing relative strength. For example, sectors sensitive to changes in interest rates tend to anticipate both the minimums and the maximums.

The sectors sensitive to the demand for capital goods or raw materials generally tend to follow the market's overall trend with delay. Through ETFs, it is possible to immediately position on a specific stock without necessarily being forced to buy the different securities belonging to that particular basket. It will be possible to obtain immediate exposure to this sector, benefiting from its value growth, besides the advantages linked to the diversification.

It is also possible to invest using relative strength, investing, perhaps, on a stock exchange index while benefiting from its growth in value and the advantages linked to diversification.

For example, if one thinks that the US market should grow in relative terms at a given moment to a greater extent than the French one, it will be appropriate to make the first one and underweight the second one.

This decision can be reached by analyzing the relative comparative strength between the two markets, which compares two dimensions (composed of market, sector, securities, or other indices) to show how these values are performing comparably. Respect for each other. The trend changes expressed by relative strength generally tend to anticipate the actual ones of the financial activity to which it refers. Therefore, it is possible to use the relative strength to direct purchases towards ETFs that show a growing relative force.

ETFs' high flexibility also allows the construction of guaranteed capital investment; in times of financial turbulence, investors often turn to products that provide capital protection: those provided by financial intermediaries often have high charges for customers. It is possible to build a guaranteed capital product by yourself, which respects your personal investment needs. The central point of the logic of guaranteed capital is interest rates and the duration of the investment. At the base of all, there are central concepts of finance: the higher the interest rates, the greater the return on the money as the duration increases, you earn more because money "works" longer.

In many years, the money we will obtain can be brought to today, as for bills that follow the discount law (the technical term of bringing the future money to today). You can quickly answer the question: "to have 100$ in seven years, knowing that the rates are at 5%, how much money do I have to invest?" This statement indicates how much money is needed to invest today to get the desired amount at maturity.

The bonds that allow only the fruits to maturity, without paying interest during their life, are called zero-coupon bonds (zcb) and are quite common on the market. If for example, I want to have $100 at maturity and interest rates are at 5% I will have to invest in zero-coupon bonds $95.24 (if the deadline is between one year) $78.35 (if the deadline is in five years) $61.39 (if the deadline is ten years) €48.1 (if the deadline is between fifty years) and $23.21 (if the deadline is thirty years)

In effect, by building investment with guaranteed capital, one only has to decide how to invest the remaining part of the initial $100 that have not been allocated in the zero coupons. An ideal solution could be to invest in options because they can amplify any yield thanks to the leverage effect. If you have a less aggressive investment profile, ETFs are excellent tools to build guaranteed capital investment. If, for example, we assume a ten-year investment with rates of 2.5% for that maturity, the portion to be invested in zcb is equal to 78.12%. In comparison, the remaining 21.88% will be invested in the ETF.

This investment strategy achieves a minimum (not real) "money" return target with few operations, as the zcb provides for the repayment only on the nominal amount of the loan (not discounted to the inflation rate). Therefore, it is a valid methodology for those who intend to make investments with clear objectives and have little time to devote to monitoring the values as only an operation until expiry may be necessary.

Unlike a guaranteed capital product offered by any financial intermediary, an investment of this kind built independently with ETFs can be dismantled entirely or in pieces (selling only the zcb or existing assets, ETF) to meet any need.

Naturally, only at maturity will there be a certainty of the pre-established return and, throughout the loan, a temporary adverse trend in financial variables, (rates rise by lowering the zcb and at the same time decreasing the value of the ETF) could result in the liquidation of losing positions. The same consequence would be selling a structured bond, with the advantage that "doing it at home," the commissions are much lower. You can separate the two components and, if necessary, liquidate only one, according to specific needs.

The Profitability of Equity (Roe)

This is the ratio between the net result and a given company's net assets. Mainly from equity investments is an essential parameter as profitability higher than the cost of capital is an index of an enterprise's ability to create value. Therefore, it should guarantee a higher capacity for the securities' growth in the phases of the rise of the market and resistance in the reflexive phases. From this point of view, the Roe is always held in strong consideration by those who choose to invest in shares today.

Price/Earnings Ratio

A low ratio of this parameter makes a share price particularly attractive, but at the same time, it could mean that expectations regarding future profits are not particularly positive. As in the Roe case, this is a factor to be taken into due consideration when choosing the best actions to invest in.

Price-Book Value Ratio

It is the share price and the net asset value resulting from the last balance sheet, especially if this ratio is lower than the unit, which means that the company is being paid less than the value of the net budget liabilities. However, this does not necessarily mean that it is a good deal since it may not produce profits.

Dividend Yield

This is the percentage ratio between the last distributed dividend and the share price. In particular, it measures the company's remuneration to shareholders in the last year in the form of liquidity. This parameter is often taken into account to identify the securities to invest in since a company that can distribute dividends is generally a good company.

In this case, as with all the other selection parameters, it is necessary for a broader and more complete analysis since a high level of this indicator could also mean that the company has made few investments or has little prospect of growth. For this reason, looking at the dividend yield as a primary factor in determining the securities to invest in the options market is reductive. The dividend yield only makes sense if accompanied by considerations of the listed company's business plans and industrial plans.

CHAPTER 13:

Charts to Assist With the Explaining

Graphs that are used to analyze technical analysis are commonly referred to as charts. The technical analysis charts used in the financial markets tend to identify two major components in trading. They narrow down to depicting the trends and patterns that are being experienced in foreign exchange markets. Other chart functions are used in the process of an individual trying to understand the financial markets. It can be hard to interpret the graphs for an individual who is a beginner in the financial markets.

There several forms of graphs that are used in the current world to analyze financial markets technically. However, three common graphs are heavily relied on by traders in this sector of trading. These charts include candlesticks, line charts, and graphs. There is a common similarity that is shared across the three graphs. They are all created by the use of the same price data. However, the difference crops in when it comes to the displaying of data. All three graphs have a different way in which they display the data.

The difference between major types of graphs makes a trader have varied forms of technical analysis.

However, the graphs have various advantages that they present to a trader investing their time and resources in financial markets. They help a trader to make informed decisions about the market. The advantages and uses of technical analysis graphs can be effectively used in the trade of options. These analyzing graphs include:

Line Charts

This form of type of graphs is common in financial markets. It is common for people who are known for trading stock. However, this analysis graph's fame and advantage have led it to be used in the trade of options. This sector of financial trading has also proved to be effective in the roles it is tasked with. People who are beginners in options trading and other forms of financial trading are always encouraged to use this graph because one can easily understand it.

It is easy for someone to interpret this graph because it focuses on the market holistically. This helps to eliminate the shifts in data that proves to be a heavy task for various people. Emotions are always put aside because this form of analysis uses factual figures presented to it.

What this graph simply does is illustrating the display are the closing prices. There is nothing else that is portrayed in the line charts. Each of the portrayed closing prices tends to be linked to the closing price seen in the last trading session. This makes a continuous line that flows easily. This type of graph has places that easily depict it. They are popular in several web articles, newspapers, and television programs. It is because several people can easily digest them. The graph provides an individual with less amount of information to handle. This is completely different from those bar charts or candlesticks. One can describe the graph as having a simplistic view of the market with just a simple glance.

Something is intriguing when it comes to this graph's advantage of helping an individual manage their emotions. The process of trading is done by humans characterized by having feelings attached to what they do. These emotions are drawn away by the usage of neutral colors. Several choppy movements have easily eliminated the usage of several colors.

Bar Graphs (OHLC)

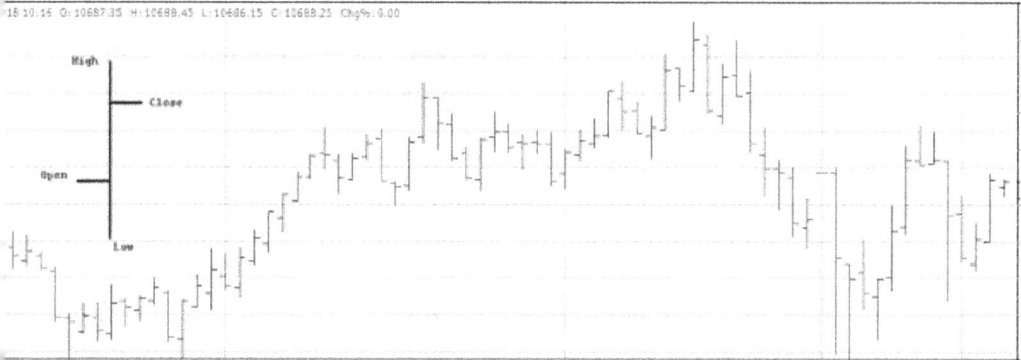

Individuals who commonly trade options that involve commodities as the underlying assets are commonly known to use this graph. It is very popular because of its effectiveness in the financial markets, and its success is vastly experienced in trading stock options and foreign exchange markets. An individual at the intermediate level of options trading will be advantaged to using this graph while studying the market. There is a unique way by which this graph analyses the trends in the market. The data collected on the prices of financial instruments help to sport the trend in the market. They help in the identification of the entry and support or resistance points in the trade of options. The advantage with this graph is it's detailed hence giving added information to a trader.

This bar graph can display closing, opening, high, and low prices for specific periods designated in the bar. The high and low prices in the graph create the vertical line of the graph. There are always two dashes that are present in the graph. The one on the left always signifies the signals of closings price while the one on the right signifies the opening prices' signals. There is a similarity that is presented between this kind of graph and candlestick. Both graphs are easily viewed on the sides though the bar graph tends to have a clearer view.

Candlesticks Charts

Some individuals are used for trading in the financial markets to use this graph to analyze the options markets. They can be equated to the bar graphs since they are commonly preferred by intermediate traders in the trade of options. Candlestick can look easier in a trader's eye compared to bar graphs because of their full nature.

A candlestick graph does a function of displaying the opening, closing (OHLC), low, and high prices for the period that is designated for each candle. The candle body of each stick represents the opening and closing prices. On the other side, the candle wicks tend to signify the high and low prices for each specific period. Several colors are used in this graph, which is green and red. The green color represents the prices closing high than when they were opened. On the other hand, the red color signifies the prices closed low than when they were opened.

CHAPTER 14:

Common Options Trading Mistakes

No one can claim to be the perfect trader. We all make mistakes, even the best of us. When we note our mistakes and admit to them, we get a chance to become better. Some mistakes are often repeated over and over again, yet they can be avoided. There are, however, some general mistakes that you need to avoid if you are to trade options successfully:

Trading Without a Definite Exit Plan

You need to learn how to control your emotions as a trader. This is true whether you are trading in stocks or options. You always need to have a plan, work with the plan, and stick to it no matter your feelings. An exit plan is necessary whether you are losing or winning. In short, have an upside exit point and a downside exit point.

Trying to Make Up for Losses Incurred

Most traders will lose money at one point or another. This is a common occurrence. However, many beginners or rookie traders often get into a panic after losing money. Inexperienced traders often panic after losing a couple of trades and will try and pump in more money in a panic. You should not do this as it will only cost you more money. Instead, take a deep breath, relax, and even take a break.

Sometimes, traders tend to double up, a way of investing more money in trades in their attempt to recoup their losses. While this can be a tempting affair, you should learn to avoid and stick to your investment plan. Your plan is very important and will guide all your online trading ventures.

Not Performing Sufficient Research on a Position

You have to conduct due diligence and do your homework. If you do not use the tools provided, study charts, compare performance, and lots of other things that you should, then your trades may not be successful. You will only lose money and not even have a chance to understand why. Ensure that you put in the work necessary and work hard so that you can trade successfully. An informed trader is most often a successful trader and vice versa.

Trading With a Fixed Mind

Many traders often trade with a fixed mind, thinking they are always right. Sometimes, even when evidence is available to the contrary, traders still stick to their positions. Instead of insisting on being right, the focus should be on being profitable, and this means being flexible and having an open mind.

Waiting a Long Time to Buy Back Short Strategies

As a trader, you need always to be ready to purchase short strategies and do so early enough. Sometimes, when a trade happens profitably, and according to your wishes, you may tend to relax. You may form an opinion that this run will continue forever. Such trades or runs can easily change direction.

Should a short option that you have goes out-of-the-money, then you should buy it back. If you can manage to rescue over 80% of your earlier gains, you should buy back the option.

Purchasing Out-of-the-Money Options

Some of the cheapest options in the options market are the out-of-money options. Many beginners often rush to buy these because of their low cost, and this might seem like, therefore, to them. However, there is a reason these options are so cheap. Most of them have very little chance of ending up in-the-money, so that they may be worth nothing eventually.

If you are to purchase these options, you have to be accurate in terms of time and direction. You will still lose out even if the direction is accurate if you sit on them too long. The expiration date is often the most crucial determinant about whether the options will finish in-the-money.

To fix this, try and go for straight long puts and calls. Get these in-the-money options as soon as possible. While they are likely to be more expensive, they possess a better chance of success and will likely earn you a profit.

Letting Short Options Go Unmonitored

One of the most outstanding features of short options is that they carry limited rewards and unlimited risks. While this might be a turnoff to some investors, it should not deter you. Short options can be a very lucrative way of getting an income. However, as a trader, you have to remain in-charge and involved.

You should monitor both the upside and downside of this option and see how it is performing. Many traders, however, try to get as much out of their options as possible. This might see them end up in a loss. The best approach with short options is never to let them go in-the-money. That is unless they are covered calls or when you are applying puts to find stocks. Also, ensure to set your points where you will exit. It could be determined by a maximum loss amount or your technical analysis of the trades.

Trading Low-Volume Options

One of the important factors of options trading is dealing with liquid options. Liquidity here stands for the speed at which you can enter or exit a given position at a desirable price. If the liquidity is low, then the chance of exiting at your preferred time or price is limited.

Remember that just because options are listed on the market does not imply that they are good for trading. Most listed options will not be traded. Smaller companies do not have liquid options. Try and avoid being so far out-of-the-money or even in-the-money.

Not Being Informed as You Trade

It is very crucial that when you start trading, you have all the necessary information, so you make the correct and informed decisions. However, not being informed is a problem experienced not just by rookie traders but even experienced ones. Remember the part about doing your homework? This is very important.

You should always keep abreast of matters about macro and micro-economics. Also, make sure to have the economic calendar to know when a major economic news item is to be announced. Such information is definitely important and will help guide you even as you make your trades' financial decisions.

At a micro-level, you want to look at a company's information. For instance, do they have any major impending announcements? Major announcements can have a great impact on the stock exchange. Stocks may rise drastically or drop significantly. It is okay to trade, but you should have sufficient knowledge to understand how they affect your overall trading strategy.

Trading Options Without Properly Understanding Them

Plenty of beginners often lack a deeper understanding of options. For instance, a trader purchases a call stock option when the share experiences a price increase, but the option loses money. This usually happens due to the volatility of the stocks. It also goes to show the lack of a deeper understanding of stock options.

You don't need to understand every minute detail before you embark on your trades. You need to have at least some basic information about the company whose stocks you are about to deal in. You also need to understand how different stock trading strategies can benefit you and how each strategy reacts to time, direction, and volatility.

Understand a Strategy Before Implementing It

Most advanced traders venture into advanced options trading by implementing intermediate strategies that involve a combination of strategies. There is nothing wrong with this, and it is a good approach. First trades should not be complicated and should not be within an iron condor. The only issue here is that, as a trader, you may get stuck into these strategies and forget that there are many other great strategies out there. If you do not diversify your strategies, then you may lose out.

In options trading, traders can move in any direction and leverage the market. For instance, options can allow you to trade profitably whether the market is volatile or not, is moving upwards, is on a downward trend, or is not moving at all. A good trader can exploit all these different market situations to ensure that they can benefit from them and maximize their profits.

However, not all strategies will work for everyone or in all situations. However, by venturing out with knowledge and understanding, it will be possible to eventually identify the kinds of strategies that work for you in every different situation. Strategies can be tried in small sizes after a proper understanding of how they function.

Conclusion

Options trading is a form of financial speculation that allows investors to buy or sell stock options without owning the underlying stock. This tends to result in much higher returns than investing in stocks directly.

One of options trading's biggest benefits is that it does not require a great deal of initial capital. Even a small sum can be used to buy stock options. However, the cost can quickly add up if large quantities are traded. The monthly premium will need to be paid using the profits generated when the option is exercised.

The basic principle of options trading is that an asset's price can rise or fall in a given time frame. It is a strategy of hedging your position in the market by purchasing a call or put option, which provides you with the right to sell or buy an asset at a specified price, respectively. You also have the right to buy or sell an option at a set price within a set time frame. There are only two types of options at *Options Trading for Beginners*, calls, and puts.

Options trading is thought to be the more sophisticated form of investing because it allows you to trade for price moves rather than simply for the stock itself. It requires more knowledge and understanding of the market.

To use options trading, you must predict how a stock or index will move in the future and what the potential price range is for that move. The more information you learn, the better you'll be able to predict these movements and buy a call or put options accordingly.

Trading options is one way to profit when a stock goes up or down, but it isn't the only option available. You can take positions without using any of your capital by simply buying puts or calls on a stock you want to own. You can sell puts when you think there will be a downward price movement, and you can sell calls when you believe the price will go up.

Although it might sound complicated, options trading is very straightforward and can be learned quickly with a little guidance from professional traders.

With options, there are several different trading platforms and strategies you can choose from. You must choose the type of trading which suits your personality the most.

If you're a beginner or live in an area with high stock market volatility, then I'd recommend that you stick to only index options and invest in only stocks for a while. This way, you can test out your options trading capability without the added risk of losing your money.

It is highly recommended that you read this guide and make some notes to learn more about options trading. This will help you understand it better and avoid common mistakes.

www.ingramcontent.com/pod-product-compliance
Lightning Source LLC
Chambersburg PA
CBHW071718210326
41597CB00017B/2520